WITH EVERY DAMN BRICK

DISCOVER HOW TO STAND IN YOUR POWER, LIVE YOUR AUTHENTIC TRUTH & CREATE THE LIFE OF YOUR DREAMS

Rochelle Okoye

PROMINENCE PUBLISHING

Disclaimer: Names and places have been changed to protect the identities of certain individuals that are mentioned in the book. This publication is designed to provide entertainment and educational information with regard to the subject matter covered. It is sold with the understanding that the publisher is not engaged in rendering legal, accounting, or other professional advice. If professional advice or other expert assistance is required, the services of a competent professional should be sought. The opinions expressed by the author of this book are not endorsed by Prominence Publishing and are the sole responsibility of the author rendering the opinion.

Published by Prominence Publishing
www.prominencepublishing.com

Quantity sales: Special discounts are available on quantity purchases by corporations, associations, and others. For details, contact the publisher.

With Every Damn Brick/Rochelle Okoye. -- 1st ed.

ISBN: 978-1-988925-36-3

*A successful person is someone who can build
a solid foundation with the bricks
others have thrown at them.*

Table of Contents

Perseverance 1

Openness 33

Willingness 47

Evolve 65

Responsibility 81

About the Author 105

my experience
overcoming the situation
Injury
emotion/spiritual
Me
Harsh realities

CHAPTER ONE

Perseverance

Once upon a time in December 2014, my spirit, body, and mind had fallen into an uncomfortable and rather dark place. I was depressed, alone, scared and I couldn't see the light at the end of the tunnel. I was contemplating ending my life. At the time, I had sustained a near career-ending injury that left me on permanent disability with an ankle that did not allow me to function as I once did. I was caught up in an abusive and hurtful romantic relationship. I had been disowned and abandoned by my biological parents and family nine years prior. I felt like I had nobody in my darkest of times, nobody to turn to, nobody to lean on, and nobody who could help me. That being said, by no means do I mean to discredit, diminish or dishonor the loyal friendship between my best friend and me, who has been there through the thick of it all for the past 14 years; sometimes near, sometimes far. I am immensely and eternally grateful for our friendship. However, despite having this friendship and support in my life, I still felt alone, afraid, hurt, abandoned, heartbroken, lost, and confused. These were adversities that were handed to me to face on my own. I had to learn to fight, to stand on my own two feet, fully, in my divine feminine power and brave this harsh world.

At this particular time, I could not see my future. I thought if I could not fulfill doing my passion or what I thought I was put here to do, then what is the point of being here? I thought I knew it all and had it all figured out. I thought I was aware of what my soul's true purpose was. Apparently, I thought wrong.

my mindframe before when I first injuring myself

Have you ever heard of the expression, "We make plans and then God laughs?" Well, I learned this the hard way. As it turned out, I had no idea that my soul's purpose was not yet fully revealed to me. I had to keep experiencing life and overcoming adversity before I could fully discover it.

April 1, 2013, ironically also known as April Fool's Day; the sun was shining, and it was a beautiful clear morning. I was headed to set to work on a popular television show, thinking to myself, *Today will be an easy day! And next week, I'll be on a plane to stunt double for one of Hollywood's biggest movie stars, Halle Berry, on X-Men: Days of Future Past and get to tick one of my goals off my vision board.*

I arrive at work, sign in, and I am put through the works: hair, make up, and wardrobe. I get called to set, and when I arrive, my stunt coordinator explains the specific stunt that is required of me. There were some elements that I was not comfortable with but when I voiced my concerns regarding my safety, unfortunately, they were not considered.

At the time I was put in a rather difficult and uncomfortable position that I, as a stunt performer, sometimes have to face. However, being a newer performer at that time in my career, I wasn't really sure what the outcome would be with me taking a stand and saying, "No!" I chose fear over my authentic truth. I was not fully standing in my power and confident with my voice.

→ ME!

Instead, I chose to say "yes," knowing full well that the consequence may not be in my favor. I linked arms with my two male co-workers as the director prepared to yell Action. When we heard the magic words, we began running; I was in the middle and each co-worker linked on either side of me. We bolted full speed down the dock and jumped off it, landing approximately 14 feet below onto a mat that was floating on the ocean. The problem was, I was performing this stunt in 3-4" heels, and I was required to land on my feet. As you can imagine, when I landed, reaffirming the concern I had voiced, I heard my ankle pop and snap. I immediately felt an intensely painful burning sensation shoot up my leg. I thought right there and then it was broken in half. I was carried up the ladder, back to dry land with the sensation of my ankle on fire. I have a very high threshold for pain, but this burned and ached like never before. I managed to counter the pain with deep breaths of disbelief and the occasional disheartened laughter. I was carried to the ledge by my stunt coordinator and assessed by the medic. My ankle had rolled over so far and taken such a brunt force on impact from the height I had jumped, that the buckle on the outside of my boot had cut through the leather and cut me directly across my ankle. My boot was cut off my ankle; the director apologized, informed me they got the shot, and I was rushed to the hospital. I ended up tearing all three ligaments in my right ankle, compressing my talus into my tibia, and my joint locked up.

In the end, and a month later, I regretfully and sadly had to give up my stunt doubling job for Halle Berry on X-Men, as the complexity of the injury I had sustained ended up taking two years before I could return to the stunt world. Two years of surgery. Two years of physiotherapy and manual rehabilitation. Two years of cognitive therapy. Two more years of trying to keep my head above water - learning how to mourn the life I thought I was meant to have and accept the life I had been given. Two painful and challenging years of learning to overcome another adversity taught me that much more about perseverance, strength, and resiliency.

During this experience, there were many moments when I wanted to give up, but I chose not to. In those moments when I thought I could not go on, I did. In those moments I was walking through hell, I kept going. And before I knew it, weeks turned into months, months turned into years, and I learned how to walk, run, and jump again. I saved my life, and I fought for my career, and I got it back!

In March 2015, I received the call to return to the Franchise for X-Men: Apocalypse and offered the opportunity to stunt double as Storm. I also booked an action actress role as the character Famine. I took the job with immense gratitude and saw it as coming full circle. I had come so far in what seemed like forever. Looking back in hindsight, it was merely a fraction. A fraction of time that served me to my highest even if, at the time, it felt like I was in hell and enduring so much heartbreak and pain. Winston Churchill once said, "If you are going through hell, keep going." I wrote that quote on my mirror, and I read it every single day, I chose to do the work and to keep going, to keep walking through hell; to fight to get out, to save my life and to get my career back.

In those painful and confusing moments, I had two choices: I could be the victim or the victor of my story. I had a choice—give up and end it all or continue fighting in the hopes that I could come out of this with lessons learned and applied. I hoped that I would be able to find the blessings in the lessons; after all, that is the miracle in overcoming your adversities. We all have a choice to be the victim or victor of our stories and throughout your life, there will come a time when you realize that no one is coming to save you, and you must save yourself.

Become Your own SUPERHERO

I learned that several years prior to this injury and event, and I was to be taught by the Universe how to become my own superhero through the challenges I would be presented within this lifetime. Every great story has a great conflict that has been overcome.

In May 2015, I returned to Montreal and completed my job on X-Men: Apocalypse successfully. I was able to test my new limits with my newfound ankle. To this day, the injury left me with no longer having functional range of motion, which means that I have lost 50% range of motion in my right ankle, which is essential for being able to do what I used to be able to do. I experience chronic pain every day and am consciously aware of it at all times. However, on this job, I was able to discover that I did not need what I once had in order to continue succeeding in my career. I discovered just how much strength, courage, and bravery I had within my soul. I had always known I have a warrior spirit, but this journey further proved it to me. I learned who my real friends were and the people who truly have my back. People genuinely reveal their true character when you have nothing to offer them. I learned new insight, wisdom, and knowledge from overcoming something life-changing and painful. I became a walking example that you can fall on your face and everything can be taken away, but you have a choice to allow it to define you or to allow it to build you and help you grow. In going through all of my hardships and challenges, I've learned that choosing to be the victor will serve you much greater in the long run and put you on the path to becoming the best version of yourself and living your authentic truth. I will touch more on this in chapter 5.

Rule number one to overcoming adversity and standing in your power is to persevere always, no matter what. Perseverance is the steadfastness in doing something despite difficulty or delay in achieving success.

Let's face it. We've all been there to some extent: heartbroken, lost, confused, alone, and hurt. Maybe you can't seem to land that job or maybe you're not quite accomplishing the goals you've set out for yourself in the desired time you had set. Maybe you just got out of a really painful relationship or can't seem to get into the one you think you want. Whatever it might be, you keep feeling like the weight of the world is riding on your shoulders, and everything seems to be falling apart or going against you. All these emotions of sorrow, pain, hurt, despair, they're too much to bear, and you're sick and tired of being sick and tired.

Your soul may feel exhausted; you might need some retreat, some love, and some peace. In these moments, take a deep breath, relish and feel comforted in the idea and knowledge that the Universe, God, Angels, and your Spirit Guides have your back and are near and here for you. Before you close the book or run away because I used the terms God, Angels and Spirit Guides, hear me out. Perhaps you're not a spiritual or religious person so those terms may not resonate with you, but that's okay! We all have different perspectives and conscious awareness when it comes to religion and spirituality. We will all believe and perceive things differently depending on each of our respective individual journeys and experiences in this lifetime.

One of the beautiful parts of being human is that we all have the free will to believe in whatever we choose. There is no judgment there. Whether or not you choose to believe in God, Jesus, Allah, A Higher Energy Source, Creator, the Universe, Your Higher Self, Spirit Guides, Angels, or whatever you'd like to call it, it's up to you. It all refers back to source or to love. As Rumi states, "We are born of love, love is our mother." Therefore regardless of our differences and upset in the world, at the root of it all, we all believe in love, we are born from it. After all, in the end, love will save us all. Love is source, Love is the Universe, Love is God, Love is life and in saying that the reverse is true. Source is Love, the Universe is Love, God is Love and Life is Love. For the purpose of this book, I will be referring to source as God and the Universe but you can feel free to replace the words I use with whatever aligns with your soul.

We, as humans, all operate and function according to our own free will. Our free will is the choice to participate in a certain situation, engage in a certain manner, believe a certain thought, or behave in a certain way, etc. Essentially, free will is your choice to function and think how you see fit as a human, here on this earth plane. Throughout the book, you will learn just how important and how much free will plays in our ability to stand in our power.

There is a very basic formula set in place that every human being and soul has access to, which has widely become known as 'The Law of Attraction.' Maybe this is a new term to you, or maybe you've heard of it before. The Law of attraction, when put into action, essentially is a formula within the Universe that allows you or me to manifest whatever our hearts and souls desire, whatever it is, both positive and/or negative. But in order to apply the formula, first you have to believe there is a formula that exists and that you have the power to find the answer to it. In short, you have to believe in yourself and believe you have the power to create the life of your dreams.

Prior to my film career, well over 15 years ago, I wasn't a whole-hearted believer in God. I was unsure about the whole concept of the Universe, and our souls and beings vibrating on different vibrational frequencies, both positive or negative. I didn't understand that everything was made up of energy. I didn't fully understand the term consciousness or mindfulness. I hadn't yet been introduced to the concept of 'the Law of Attraction.' The famous book that brought it back to light in modern times, The Secret, hadn't been published yet.

I had endured a life of abuse, and my parents had disowned me, and with that came deep-seated wounds of abandonment, aloneness and fear. I was enrolled in private school most of my life growing up and force-fed Christianity from birth. I was an altar girl and attended church every Sunday. I was trying to figure it all out on my own, as many of us do. It wasn't until a few years prior to embarking on my film career that I started opening up to my spiritual essence and higher self. As I mentioned earlier, we are all on a different level in our spiritual journeys and we all operate from different levels of consciousness depending on what we've been through in our respective journeys and what we've learned and applied to our lives along the way. For some, you are further along the attunement of your higher selves, and for others, you are just now waking up to the fact that you are the creator of your own reality and coming to know or become aware of your higher self.

Your higher self exists in a state of love. Every time you are loving, kind, forgiving, and compassionate to yourself and others, you're being your higher self. Learn to love everything in your life, every thought, every feeling, and every action you take. Think of yourself as a beautiful, loving person, doing the best you know in order to grow. No matter where you are on your journey, as long as you are continually trying to learn, love and evolve then you are on the right path and aligned with love and your higher self.

The harsh reality is sometimes people will throw bricks at you. Sometimes the people who you thought would never dare to hurt you can throw those bricks really hard and end up hurting you the most. People you love. People you care about deeply. People whom you would go to war for and never ever consider hurting in return. Every brick serves as a metaphor for life's challenges being served up and handed to you. I say being served up, because that's exactly what's happening. The Universe oftentimes creates situations, events, adversities, hardships and or challenges in order for you to ascend into your highest self, into the best version of yourself, living and breathing your authentic truth. If only you could see the magic that is unfolding behind the veils in the Universe, you would understand that everything is happening for you and not against you. Never give up. Just because you can't see what the Universe is conspiring for you, doesn't mean it's not happening. Be patient. Everything happens in the right time.

When you can start to shift your perspective into knowing this, you will begin to observe your external world and feel your internal world change for the better.

I could build a castle out of all the bricks they threw at me. And metaphorically speaking, I did. When I look around now, I see a firm foundation that I laid with the bricks others have thrown at me. It took time, it took enduring a lot of pain, and it took forgiveness and healing. It took a lot of labor and self-love to complete the foundation. But once completed, I started building my castle and empire with all of the bricks others had thrown.

As I mentioned earlier, your adversities don't happen to you, they happen for you. And we all have the choice to be the victim or victor of our stories. And as I've mentioned before, I've been there. It can be so incredibly painful! When you're feeling down in the dumps it's easy to have negative self-talk and get caught up in always feeling bad, which in turn can lead to depression and even worse, suicide. But what if you became aware of the fact that that inner dialogue you're having with yourself is a part of what's preventing you from feeling better and from getting out of that downward spiral? What if I told you that what we put out to the Universe is what we get sent back? Would you become more conscious of your inner dialogue, thoughts, and feelings?

The Law of Attraction is:

Your Action + Your Thoughts = Your Outcome.

We are spiritual beings having a human experience, whether you choose to believe that or not. We are all made up of energy. Essentially we are souls existing in flesh vessels. Everything in this Universe is made up of energy. Science now explains this clearly and concisely. Negative thoughts, words and emotions attach themselves to a negative vibrational frequency. So when you think, speak or feel something negative, you're emitting a negative vibrational frequency out to the Universe. When the Universe feels this negative vibration that you are emitting, it will mirror that and reflect it back to you. In this particular case, it will be something negative. However, if you think, speak or feel something positive, then you are emitting a positive vibrational frequency out into the Universe and in turn the Universe will mirror back to you something positive. So if you want to start manifesting your desires and dreams you have to start thinking and feeling positive thoughts surrounding it.

Dealing with a near career-ending injury that changed my life in the blink of an eye, having minimal to no love or support through the process from family or loved ones, all while enduring and being in an abusive romantic relationship, personally left me feeling completely broken, lost, and unsure of where to go next and how to carry on with what I had left. It proved to be a very difficult chapter that I had to experience.

When I was completely shattered and had nowhere to go, I sought answers I didn't have and I felt the need to pray. I prayed to the Universe and to God every day, even in those moments when I didn't have the energy or the strength to feel good about it. I would still pray. Because when you pray, you're emitting a positive frequency. You are coming from a place of surrender and love, rather than ego. The Universe loves it when you come from a place of love and can let go of your ego. Through the answers I sought, I chose to write down positive affirmations on all of my mirrors. Any time I passed by them, I forced myself to read the quote reflecting back at me, even if I didn't fully believe in what I was reading at the time. My mind was trained otherwise and was experiencing symptoms of depression. Regardless of how I was really feeling, I would still force myself to say those positive affirmations, knowing full well that, one day, even if I didn't believe it then, I would trick my brain into believing it and feeling it, simply because I was repeating it daily. I understood that eventually I would encompass it with all my heart and all my soul.

Buddha said, "The mind is everything; what you think, you become." That quote really resonated with me when I was finding myself and embarking on my film career. I have carried it with me and used it in my daily repertoire of life mottos to this day.

Essentially, I was training my brain to believe it was healing my body, to believe I would walk again, to believe I would get my career back, to believe that I would find the lesson in all of this and understand the 'why', and to believe that I would persevere. I prayed, and I worked very hard to get whatever physical function I could get back from my ankle and to return to my career. Remember when I said, The Law of Attraction is: Your Action + Your Thoughts = Your Outcome? The second part of that is Action. You have to show the Universe your new vibrations. It's not just enough to pray and ask for it. You also have to show up and do the work, which is also your part of the deal.

The medical community and surgeons repeatedly told me that my healing would not happen, that I may never walk properly again, let alone get my career back. Despite the naysayers and doubters, I chose to refuse to believe them. At that time, I was fully aware that I was the creator of my own reality, and nobody could tell me or dictate what I was and wasn't capable of attaining or getting back. Some call me stubborn; I like to think of it as strength and power.

I couldn't walk, run or jump. I was wheelchair bound and then on crutches for 6 months. I worked diligently morning, afternoon and night, going from rehab, to strength and conditioning with my kinesiologist, to 3 different physiotherapists all over the city, to 3 different massage therapists, to my naturopath, to my doctor, to my 2 surgeons and back again for 2 years nonstop, every single day except Sundays! I had a massive and extremely supportive and knowledgeable rehab team all working towards the same collective goal: to get my ankle and career back. I am so eternally grateful for each and every one of them to this day. It was an extremely tiring, exhausting, challenging, painful, depressing process with a lot of lows and some highs and what felt like a roller coaster part of my journey. It was another one of my difficult challenges that I clearly had to overcome, to learn from, to evolve from, to move forward from, and to help others through communicating what I had learned from my painful experience.

I finally learned to walk on my own again after 6 months, although it was with a very severe and painful limp, and minimal range of motion. It took me 2 years to be able to run and jump again. I've been assessed and put on permanent disability until I'm 65 years old. But in saying all of that and despite what the medical community repeatedly told me, I got my career back. It didn't slow down; it just changed respectively to accommodate my new injury. I was and am still presented with amazing opportunities. Some I take; others I'm not able to for various reasons, and I'm content with that. I've learned that what's meant to be will be, and I'm okay with saying, no! Overall, I'm still learning to adapt; in fact, it's been a continual 5-year journey of learning to adapt and attune to my new body and ankle, learning my new limits and playing within them. It forced me to slow down at the time and to learn to stop and smell the roses. We get so caught up in thinking we have to be constantly working or grinding in order to be successful. We forget to embrace the concept that rest, recovery, and reflection are essential parts of the progress towards a successful and ultimately happy life. I chose not to listen to my intuition, to my higher self, to my body the day I jumped off the dock. And as a result, the Universe and my higher self decided it was time to teach me a valuable and detrimental lesson for my being's ascension along my journey. The Universe forced me to slow down. It's a learning process. I learned that life and success is not about the destination, it's about the journey. And on my particular journey I had to learn that valuable lesson the hard way. And for me, that's okay, that's how it had to be, that's how I chose it to be.

At the end of it all, I can stand here and tell you genuinely how grateful I am for the experience, for the downfall, and for the outcome. Yes, I would love to have a fully functioning foot, along with all of my old skill sets and abilities, BUT would I trade that for the woman I've become today? For the invaluable lessons I've learned along the way? Hell No! Not even for a minute. You see, the growth and the blessings you'll receive from overcoming your adversities far exceed what you had to lose in order to gain it. Through hardship, I learned so much about myself and about others. The wisdom, the insight, could only be gained from the experiences I had to go through. One of the many Buddhist proverbs reads, "Experience is the mother of all wisdom." I had that particular proverb tattooed on my ribs years prior to my ankle injury as a reminder that life, people, and our experiences are our University and greatest teachers. These experiences allow lessons that inevitably serve you to your highest good along the way. Lessons that allow you to continue to evolve into a human that you are proud of being and becoming. Lessons that continue your soul's evolution of becoming an unconditionally loving human being. So, thank the Universe and God for allowing the experience to happen and for providing the resiliency to rise above it.

Gratitude is the quality of being thankful. You cannot expect to manifest your dreams and skip the important step of encompassing gratitude for all things. You must openly be thankful for it all, the good and the bad. You can't have one without the other; everything is balance, yin and yang, light and darkness, positive and negative, duality. When you tell the Universe, "I am grateful for everything coming into my life," the Universe acknowledges that and will reflect back to you more things for you to be grateful for. Remember, the Universe is your mirror and returns to you what you put out. So, always be grateful for every blessing you receive and for every lesson and adversity that you face and overcome. In the end, it will lead you to a life filled with abundance and joy.

Faith for better days to come is another crucial part of being able to persevere so that you may learn to stand in your power and live your authentic truth.

Have faith that there is light at the end of the tunnel, and the hard times that you are facing or have faced are merely a part of your journey and not the entirety of it. This too shall pass. The bad is a part of having the good. You need the downfall in order to learn. In fact, some of our greatest lessons are learned through some of our biggest mistakes and challenges. There is much beauty to be seen in pain, and there is always a positive in a negative. Your job is to seek it, acknowledge it, and then apply it. It's important for you to be consciously aware and understand that the obstacles and challenges that are put on your path are the building blocks to being your best and reaching your highest potential. Of course everyone wants happiness. Nobody wants pain, but the fact of the matter is, you can't have a rainbow without a little rain. So, you must honor the pain, sadness, and all the negative feelings. After processing, honoring, and releasing all that no longer serves you, you now have the space to move forward with love in your heart and room to call in all the abundance and joy that will serve you to your highest and that you deserve. Have faith that the painful feeling will not last forever; it's simply referred to as growing pains. It's all a part of your soul's evolution. And it may not be up to you to fully understand 'the why?' right now, but the answers will come in time when you're ready. And when you're ready, you will know. All you have to do is ask the Universe, silence the mind, listen, be open to receiving and continue on your journey. The answers you seek will present themselves over time. You need to understand the importance of knowing that everything in our lives happens in divine order, the good, the bad, the unexpected, and the unfortunate. No matter what is in front of you, it's a part of your path. Follow, trust, believe, forgive, be grateful, and keep pushing. Persevere!

It was my faith that kept me alive during my 2 years of disability. I had faith that this was all happening for a reason. I didn't understand it at the time, but as I said, I knew one day I would. I knew it was up to my soul's growth and evolution to figure out. As long as I believed that better days were to come, and that I would rise like a phoenix from the ashes, stronger and wiser, then all would be well in the end. And that's what I maintained in my heart and in my soul, faith for better days to come.

Strength can be defined as the capacity of an object or substance to withstand great force or pressure. Also as the emotional or mental qualities necessary in dealing with situations or events that are distressing or difficult. Nobody said life was going to be easy or fair, and sometimes, it appears that some people are handed more difficult lives than others. Throughout my life and experience, I've come to realize that if your path is more difficult, it is because of your higher calling, so you must go on. You have the strength and the resiliency to fight through the tough times, to fight through the days that you feel are getting the better of you. You must hold on to that 1% of strength in you, because sometimes that's all you have, and it may be your saving life force. God will never give you an experience or adversity that you can't handle and face.

In my darkest of times with my ankle, I would constantly feel an internal pull inside of me. Sometimes barely there, but it was there. It was the strength of my soul and the will to get through it, the will to survive. Even though my brain had convinced my heart to give up, my soul eternally was strong. I affirmed; "I am Strong, I am a female warrior, and I can get through anything." I held onto that strength and affirmation for the entire journey. Especially near the end when my strength started to dwindle in the hopelessness of my ankle ever returning to 100%. Regardless, I held onto that strength, I had to, because, at one point, it felt like that's all I had.

Being a decent and loving human being is another crucial part in persevering and learning to stand in your power. Your goal while living on this Earth is to learn unconditional love and apply it to yourself and all beings across the entire Universe. Unconditional love is known as love without conditions. If you are able to love yourself, then you can love others. Know that love truly conquers all, and if you keep avoiding self-love, the Universe will keep sending you people who also avoid loving you, hoping that you get a little clue and learn your lessons. You'll stop attracting certain people and situations when you heal the parts of you that once needed them. In order to receive love, you have to be love, and that includes loving yourself above all else. You must be patient with yourself as you go through the highs and lows on your journey. Rome wasn't built in a day, and sometimes, time heals all wounds, so give time, time. Allow yourself the patience and process to grieve, to feel down, to cry, and be patient while experiencing these emotions and then love yourself enough to honor them as we spoke of before. Love yourself enough to know that you are a spiritual being, having a human experience, and feeling down is just as much a part of your journey as feeling the high and being on top of the world.

We are all human, and as such we will all fall out of alignment with love numerous times over the course of our life. The miracle is how quickly you can return back to love. Whenever I fall out of alignment with love, I check in with my higher self, and I highly recommend you do the same. Sit or lie in silence in a peaceful, safe space or practice a self or guided meditation. Silence your mind and allow whatever comes to you to come. Check in with your soul and with your inner child if appropriate. Your inner child is your childlike aspect. It includes all that we have learned and experienced as children before puberty. The inner child denotes a semi-independent entity subordinate to the waking conscious mind and is usually regarded as damaged or concealed by our negative childhood experiences. You must love yourself enough to heal your traumas, your wounds and your inner child, so that you may stand in your divine power, live your authentic truth, and create the life of your dreams.

Whenever you find yourself falling out of alignment with love, you can affirm:

> *"I love others and myself unconditionally, and the Universe reflects that back to me everywhere I go. I am full of love. I give and receive love, and I am open and grateful for receiving an abundance of unconditional love from all that is in the Universe."*

I also highly recommend the beneficial practice of journaling. Journaling provides an opportunity for healing by creating a space that allows you to put thought to paper and process that which is pouring out of you, whether it be thoughts, emotions or physical ailments. You will always benefit in a positive way from self-reflection and engaging in self-love through introspection. Introspection is the examination of one's own conscious thoughts and feelings. In psychology, the process of introspection relies exclusively on observation of one's mental state, while in a spiritual context, it may refer to the examination of one's soul. Introspection is closely related to human self-reflection and is contrasted with external observation. Love yourself enough to go within so that you can heal and ascend.

Sometimes we think holding on is what makes us strong, but sometimes it's letting go. Oftentimes we get caught up on what we think we want and what is meant for us, when in actual fact that is not our final destination, it is merely just a part of our journey. You must be willing to let go and mourn the life you planned in order to have the life that is meant for you. You cannot manifest a positive future that is yours by divine birthright if you are stuck in the hurtful past. You cannot heal in the same environment where you got sick. More often than not, the mind replays what the heart can't delete. But in order to heal your wound, you need to stop touching it. What I mean by that is, stop continually replaying that painful story over and over again. Instead, change your perception and cognition and replace negative thinking with positive affirmations and self-love. Heal, forgive and let go. Otherwise, you will only hinder your own self-growth by experiencing the same situation with a different person. The Universe tends to repeat circumstances, events, and situations until we learn the lessons we need from it.

Forgiveness plays a very important role in persevering and learning how to stand in your power. The word 'forgive' is defined in the dictionary as 'to stop feeling angry or resentful towards someone for an offense, flaw or mistake.' Forgiveness does not mean condoning the person's behavior that caused you pain. It means letting go of the hurt, the sadness, and any negative emotions, feelings and energy attached to or associated with that particular situation. Essentially, it's setting yourself free and understanding that things don't happen to you, but for you, as I mentioned earlier. In order to persevere and stand in your power so that you can live and speak your authentic truth you must forgive and let go. I will touch more on forgiveness in chapter 5.

Know that overcoming your adversities will help you master soul lessons. Overcoming your adversities will help you call in all the abundance and joy that is yours by divine birthright. So the next time you're faced with adversity and someone hits you with a brick, you must decide: victim or victor? The choice is always yours.

BASIC REVIEW

In this chapter, we looked at the first step to standing in your power, which is persevering through any adversity and challenges you may face on your journey. We looked at how you can persevere by manifesting the life you want through the Law of Attraction.

In order to persevere, we must:

1. Put in the work and have the correct and positive inner & outer dialogue when speaking to yourself, others, and the Universe.

2. We can ask for assistance, guidance, and help through prayer to the Universe, to God, to Spirit, Creator, or whatever term you choose to use that resonates with you. We can help ourselves persevere through positive affirmations.

3. Have faith when times are tough and you're in your darkest storm. Try to remember that this too shall pass; be patient with yourself and the journey.

4. Have the strength to know that you can overcome anything that you are faced with. You are a child of the Universe and a symbol of strength. Find your inner warrior and keep climbing that mountain until you reach the top.

5. Have love for yourself and for others. Understand time and love heals all wounds, so give time, time.

Honor your authentic feelings and allow them to come and go. Process them and release them with love, so you can make room for more positive and loving emotions and feelings.

6. Forgive yourself and others for any harm they may have done and any hurt they may have caused. Release them with love, so that you can release the pain and the hurt and call in all the positive things that are meant for you.

LESSON

You cannot hold onto negative vibrations and expect to call in positive things. The Universe is your mirror; what you put out, you will receive back.

There will come a time in your life when you realize that no one is coming to save you and you must save yourself. In this moment you'll have two choices; to be the victim, or to be the victor of your story.

If only you could see the magic that is unfolding behind the veils in the Universe, you would understand that everything is happening for you and not against you. Never give up. Just because you can't see what the Universe is conspiring for you, doesn't mean it's not happening. Be patient. Everything happens in the right time.

HOMEWORK

* In section A.) I want you to think about what it is you'd like to attract or manifest into your life. It can be anything, from a new apartment, the love of your life, more money, a new job, and/or better health. Whatever it is, be specific. For example, if someone wanted to call in and meet the love of their life, he or she would write: "In the next year, I'd like to meet the love of my life and be joined in divine, unconditional love, harmony and joy for one another."

* In section B.) I'd like you to write down 5 things that you're grateful for today. When you wake up every morning from this point forward, I want you to continue this practice and write down in your journal or diary 5 things that you're grateful for. They can be the simplest things, such as: *I'm grateful the sun is shining.* Or *I'm grateful to open my eyes and be alive today,* or *I'm grateful for the flower that is growing in my garden.* Anything that comes to mind, that you feel grateful for, write down and/or speak aloud.

* In section C.), I'd like you to write down 5 positive affirmations to help call in whatever you write in section A to manifest into your life.

For example: If someone wanted to call in the love of their life, they would affirm something such as:

- I am deserving of unconditional love.

- I am loved, and I give love.

- The love of my life is now in my life.

- Love is attracted to me, and I am attracted to love.

- I love myself, and I allow myself to be loved fully.

Whatever you find resonates and/or aligns with you, write it down. I then want you to buy a whiteboard dry erase marker and write these affirmations down on your mirrors and repeat them daily. You can write them down and repeat them daily in your journal or make post-it notes and stick them where you can see them in your house or office. You can even make screenshots out of them and save them as your phone background. The idea is to see them as much as possible and repeat them as much as possible. These will become your mantras, your prayers.

* In section D.) I'd like you to write 5 Steps to action that you can do in the physical world to help manifest your dreams.

For example: Someone wanting to meet the love of his or her life would write down:

1.   I will make an effort to go out more and socialize, doing things that resonate and align with me and provide joy in my life.

2. I will be kinder and more loving to those people that I don't understand.

I want you to go out and do what you're writing down. Remember, it's not good enough just to ask the Universe for it. You must show the Universe your new vibrations and that you're making the effort and putting in the work to attain it.

A.) WRITE A SPECIFIC GOAL YOU WOULD LIKE TO ACCOMPLISH OR MANIFEST INTO YOUR LIFE.

1.

B.) WRITE 5 THINGS YOU ARE GRATEFUL FOR (REPEAT DAILY).

1.

2.

3.

4.

5.

C.) WRITE 5 AFFIRMATIONS TO CREATE A MORE POSITIVE MINDSET & ATTRACT WHAT YOU WANT (REPEAT DAILY).

1.

2.

3.

4.

5.

D.) WRITE DOWN 5 STEPS TO ACTION YOU CAN TAKE TO MANIFEST YOUR DREAM.

1.

2.

3.

4.

5.

Openness

In the fall of 2009, I started questioning if I was actually meant to be a professional boxer and world champion. To be honest, I wasn't sure if that was truly my life path. It served me well at the time, but I had always known it would not end up being my end all be all. I received a call informing me there was a role that I would be well-suited for, that I should audition and be introduced to the stunt coordinator. I auditioned. I met the stunt coordinator, who is my really good friend to this day. I booked the part, and that's when I discovered a big part of my passions and journey would entail a career in film.

I decided to retire from boxing and begin my film career full force. I had no idea what I was doing but knew that if I followed my intuition and my heart, and continued to step outside my comfort zone, that I would be led in the right direction. I picked up the book, Having it All, by John Assaraf and The Secret, by

Rhonda Byrne and they changed my perception and way of thinking at the time for the better. It started my conscious journey of manifesting my life and desires.

At that time, I had recently been abandoned and disowned by both of my parents and family and was left with an overwhelming feeling of loneliness and hurt. I thought, I don't really have much to lose, so why not try to apply what the authors in these books that I've been reading are speaking about to my life and see what happens?

I was open to trying to better myself and manifest what I wanted, and I was fully open to receiving it when the Universe presented it to me. I started using the law of attraction to manifest my goals. I used positive affirmations daily to reset my distorted perception and cognition of certain things I had learned through my abusive upbringing. I worked hard. I had worked extremely hard my whole life, with all of my athletic endeavors and accomplishments, and continued to work hard. I went to acting classes, studied more, networked, volunteered, learned what I needed, stepped outside my comfort zone, and met the people I needed to meet, and I watched my career blossom and take off rather fast. I was booking work across the country and internationally on big features and well-known television shows. And one by one, I was crossing off all the things on my vision board, and before I knew it, I had to make another one with new goals and new desires. I was ecstatic. I was creating the life I wanted, and I realized I had the power to do so.

The second step to manifesting your dreams is the genuine willingness to be open to receiving all of your blessings and lessons that the Universe will present for you.

Like me, I'm sure there has a been a time or two in your life when you have felt so heartbroken, so hopeless, and maybe like there is no light at the end of the tunnel. Our heart chakras can be so hurt and polluted with the ache of heartbreak that oftentimes it can feel closed or guarded. Sometimes, life and the people in it have burned us more often than we may like or feel we can bear. As a result, we are left protective of our hearts, fearful to let down our walls and our barriers, to assure ourselves that no one can hurt us again. But in doing so, we're actually creating the opposite of what we may wish or hope for. By remaining guarded with a blocked heart chakra, you will only repel the positive things you may be asking or hoping for. Remember the Universe is a mirror. This is why, as I explained in chapter 1, that it is essential, especially in times of despair and heartbreak, to process all of your emotions, your hurt, any negativity, and all of the heavy stuff. Once we have given ourselves the time to process and the permission to heal, we now possess the room in our hearts for all of the positive and loving energy to come through into our lives. In doing so, your heart chakra will become unblocked and open to receiving the abundance of love and joy that is yours by divine birthright.

During the process of your heart chakra becoming unblocked, you will discover that light will always win over darkness. You'll become aware that oftentimes new beginnings towards happiness don't always start happy. When you learn to come from heart center and you begin to understand all of the above, you also begin to understand the power of your being, the magic of the Universe and all it has to offer. Keeping an open heart chakra will only attract more love and empathy from others. Essentially, keeping an open heart is your statement to the Universe. A statement that reads: *I am ready to receive all that you have to offer. And I am grateful for it.* There is nothing more beautiful and empowering than that of a person with a kind, open heart and gentle soul.

Maintaining an open mind is equally as important as maintaining an open heart. In order to manifest and align with your soul's purpose, you first must believe, and in order to believe, an open mind is required. A closed mind is ignorant to all of the possibilities and magic of the Universe. We all have an infinite number of choices we can make in this lifetime, and ultimately, all choices will lead to a different outcome but each outcome can and will provide anywhere from basic to profound life lessons if you choose to learn from them.

Those that believe in the magic of the Universe are those that are open to receiving the bountiful gifts it has to provide.

Remember, in chapter 1, when I mentioned if only you could see the magic that is unfolding behind the veils in the Universe, you would understand that everything is happening for you and not against you? In order to believe this statement and have it resonate and align with your soul, you must whole-heartedly possess an open mind. Magic is all around us, patiently waiting for our senses to open and only those that believe can be open to it. With an open mind, you'll also be open to all of the beautiful and amazing possibilities that can unfold for you. On this journey of learning to stand in your power, you must harmoniously align with the Universe, so that opportunities that align with your higher purpose and goals are presented to you accordingly all in divine timing and in divine order. You can't be open to receiving something you don't believe in. So, believe, because magic is all around us. You just have to be open to it.

You'll find that once you start believing in the magic of the Universe, the Universe will start sending you signs and synchronistic activities that may provide messages, insight, answers, and proof to show you that your prayers and affirmations are being answered, that you're on the right path, to keep going, and you may even find that your desires start manifesting in the physical realm. Synchronicity is the experience of two or more events that are apparently causally unrelated or unlikely to occur together by chance yet are experienced as occurring together in a meaningful manner. You can ask the Universe at any time in your life to provide answers. You may ask the Universe to provide signs that appear in the form of something specific, such as symbols, colors, animals, numbers etc. Or you can simply ask for a sign.

A perfect example of one of the beautiful synchronicities that happened for me in my life was when I booked the role of Margaret on Fox's Wayward Pines. I really wanted this role. The character really aligned and resonated with me, and I loved the storyline and plot and had a lot of respect for all of the actors on the show. They were all well-known and extremely talented and recognized & honored for their individual work and craft. To be honest, it was a pretty weird audition, as the character was new, and they weren't really sure where they were going to go with her. She was the Queen of a tribe, where the majority was made up of all men. In a sense, I kind of created Margaret in the audition room that day. I felt like I had a really amazing audition and I felt like it went really well, but you never know with these things. Prior to entering the audition room, I prayed to my guides as I usually do, asking for their support and presence while I audition and do my thing. After the audition was complete, I expressed my gratitude for their presence and being there for me. I also asked that I let go of whatever is meant to be, and I give it to them and the Universe. But I also prayed and affirmed that I am Margaret, and that I have booked this role. I also asked my guides, if this role is meant for me, to please show me a sign in the form of a deer. I then proceeded to let it go and get on with my day. The next day, I was at home eating dinner, and I received a text from my friend. I checked it, and it was a picture of 3 deer in his yard that he felt the need to send me. I laughed warm-heartedly and expressed my gratitude to the Universe and my Guides. I replied to my friend's text, told him how beautiful the deer were and how special that moment was. Two days later, I received the call from casting that I booked the role as Margaret, Queen of the Abbies, on Fox's Wayward Pines Season 2. I was ecstatic and extremely grateful!

In saying that, you must pay attention to the synchronicities that the Universe provides for you. They are important, and they are a part of helping to guide you to what is meant for you. The more gratitude you express for the synchronicity and answers being presented, the more it will show up for you, the more you will learn, and the faster you will be standing in your power, living your authentic truth and creating the life of your dreams.

Keeping an open hand is the third and final part to remaining open in order to stand in your power and create the life of your dreams. In order to receive, you must first give. Everything in life is flow and energy.

What you give out will always come back; that is the rule of karma. And we've learned that the Universe is a mirror and will reflect back to you what you put out. If you want to accomplish your goals, it is absolutely essential to help others on their pursuit of happiness and attaining their goals as well. Rumi quotes it best, "A candle never loses its light by lighting another candle." Rumi is basically explaining by lighting the path for others, you are only creating more light. And with more light comes more possibilities, more vision, more insight, more love, more creativity, more healing and more positivity. When you give, always try to remember, to give without expectation. Meaning, give without expecting to receive anything back in return. Give graciously, unconditionally, and whole-heartedly, simply because it feels good to see the other person happy, because it lights you up inside to give a helping hand. When you give genuinely and without expectation, the Universe will recognize that and reward you for the unconditional love in your heart. Encourage and uplift others, in order to encourage and uplift yourself. The act of giving creates the same energy as the act of receiving. You are worthy of both giving and receiving love.

I got here today by helping as many people as I could along the way without expectation. Some of those people returned the favor and helped and guided me, and some could do absolutely nothing for me. But I never once cared or took that into consideration when helping others, because I give without expectation, I give with my heart, because it genuinely feels good to help others. To see other people succeed, to see their light shine, and for me to witness them embark on what lights up their soul and purpose is a beautiful gift, and that's all I could ever ask for. Remember, we rise by lifting others.

BASIC REVIEW

In this chapter, we learned that the second step to standing in your power is the ability to remain open.

1. We must keep an Open Heart - It will allow love in all aspects to flow back into our lives.

2. We must keep an Open Mind - You can only call in your desires if you believe in yourself and in the magic of the Universe.

3. We must keep an Open Hand - You must give in order to receive. The act of giving creates the same energy as the act of receiving. We rise by lifting others.

LESSON

Healing takes place when openness unconditionally and gently embraces the past.

Magic is all around; you just have to believe.

By lighting the path for others, you will also light your own path and get to your destination faster.

HOMEWORK

A.) I want you to find a dry erase marker or post-it notes, and on every mirror in your home, I want you to write down: "I am open to receiving all of the abundance from the Universe and I am grateful." Every time you pass this mirror or stand in front of it, I want you to affirm that 5x.

B.) Today, I want you to go out on your day to day activities, and I want you to engage in 5 different things that involve having an open heart, open mind, and or open hand. For example, maybe someone in the past hurt you, and you're ready to let it go to the Universe and forgive. For this exercise, maybe you can have an open heart and give to a homeless person or someone who has less than you. Whatever it is, I want you to write down the act of kindness at the end of the day in this book or your journal. And I want you to move forward in life, encompassing these values, morals and characteristics, as you walk forward on your path and journey.

1.

2.

3.

4.

5.

CHAPTER THREE

Willingness

Just when I thought things couldn't get any worse, without a doubt, they did. I made the bold choice to leave my abusive relationship with my romantic partner. You might wonder how I managed to get myself into such a relationship and predicament. Besides the fact that I was completely manipulated and blind-sided by a malignant narcissist-sociopath, I actually asked myself the same thing every day until I chose to surrender to the fact that everything happens for a reason. Oftentimes the Universe is preparing us for exactly what we asked for, therefore, every choice that we make is for a reason. We can use these experiences and these painful moments to learn from and grow or we can allow them to break us and define us. In my case, this particular painful experience and person turned out to be my worst nightmare but ultimately served me with some of my greatest lessons.

We end up in toxic relationships because we don't stand up for ourselves early on when red flags occur.

We let them slide, because we fear losing a companion. We may not fully love ourselves yet and be completely aware of our worth and value. But for how long do you let disrespect and neglect go? At some point, you have to develop healthy boundaries for how you're going to be treated; you're responsible for your experiences, nobody else is.

So here I was, a strong, independent woman, abandoned and disowned by my parents at a young age, university education and degree in tow, career driven, bringing everything to the table, supporting a man, while I was on and off of disability. I was financially, emotionally and spiritually supportive of a person who was incapable of reciprocating anything of any value or worth. Being the empath that I am, I was extremely giving of myself and of everything I had attained at this point. He chose to do nothing but ride my back, use me for everything I had and then fronted to the world like it was a part of his creation. I put a roof over his head and food on his plate without a penny from him in return. I had started a successful business, and he still chose to self-sabotage everything he had been given. He was a serial cheater, a pathological liar, and abusive in all ways. My being beside him made him look good and he was fully aware of that and in hindsight that was a part of his game in attaining what he selfishly wanted all along.

Shannon Thomas, author of Healing from Hidden Abuse[1] explains that, "narcissists, sociopaths and psychopaths are notorious for picking targets that initially boost their egos. It could be the target's appearance, age, intellect, reputation, religious convictions, career success, family, friends, or something else. Once the target is hooked, the toxic person then sets out to tear down the exact qualities that attached her or him to the survivor in the first place."

Kim Saeed, founder of the Narcissistic Abuse Recovery Program, was quoted as saying:

"When an empath and narcissist enter into a relationship together, it creates a magnetic yet dysfunctional union because the empath gives to the point of complete and utter exhaustion. Profoundly disoriented, the empath is often destroyed by the relationship. This experience is painful and overwhelming but ultimately, the empath undergoes a soul awakening. The narcissist remains the same."[2]

Healing from the abuse and trauma of this particular relationship allowed me to come to the awakening and understanding that this awful experience, these painful moments, had to happen in my life, along my journey. It catapulted me into my final stages of healing

---

[1] Thomas, S., & Choi, C. (2016). *Healing from hidden abuse: A journey through the stages of recovery from psychological abuse.* MAST Publishing House.
[2] https://kimsaeed.com

surrounding my deep-seated wounds of abandonment. I needed to go through this experience in order to attain the level of consciousness that was required of my soul in order to fulfill my soul's true purpose. I've come to understand that bad things don't happen to you, they happen for you. I've come to discover my worth and my value and through self-love and deep introspection. I learned to fully love myself right down to the very core. I now set healthy boundaries for myself. I stand fully in my divine feminine power; living, speaking and breathing my authentic truth and through it all, along the way, I discovered my soul's true purpose. I became an educated and empowered empath, which in turn also happens to be a narcissist's worst nightmare. I can happily say narcissist-sociopaths don't come for me anymore.

He happened to be my biggest mistake, but he also served as one of my greatest lessons, and I give gratitude to the Universe and God for that. I am grateful for the time we spent together, as painful as it was. He brought the lioness out of me. I fought for my life, my heart, my peace, my freedom, my healing, my soul, and my business – and I won. He freed me of my karmic debt, and the pain he caused me allowed me an opportunity to break myself open, tear myself apart, rise and ascend.

"Breaking up with a narcissist sociopath is a dark journey that will throw you into spells of depres-

sion, rage, and loneliness. It will unravel your deepest insecurities, leaving you with a lingering emptiness that haunts your every breath. But ultimately, it will heal you. You will become stronger than you could ever imagine. You will understand who you are truly meant to be."[3]

Sometimes, the most valuable and painful lessons are delivered by someone masquerading as a soul mate. I personally had a strong desire and willingness to overcome this, to survive this, and to use this to help elevate me. I had been through a lot of abuse and hardship to this point. There were great lessons to be learned here, and I knew my soul had no other choice but to learn them. Everything had to happen exactly as it did in the physical realm to awaken me to higher levels in the divine realm. Pain is meant to propel you closer to your purpose. Don't run from it. Embrace it.

In this chapter, we're going to look at how the 'willingness' to overcome your adversity and stand in your power plays an important and essential role in living your authentic truth and becoming the best version of yourself.

---

[3] MacKenzie, J. (2015). *Psychopath free: Recovering from emotionally abusive relationships with narcissists, sociopaths, and other toxic people.* New York: Berkley Books.

First, let's look at the concept of 'willpower' and how it plays a role in the 'willingness' to overcome your adversity.

Willpower is the control exerted to do something or to restrain impulses. To possess willpower is a choice. Willpower is simply a human characteristic that some of us choose to possess in the face of overcoming adversities and challenges. You cannot control your behaviour if you first cannot control your mind. In order to refrain from or overcome something, you first must believe in your mind that you are more than capable of doing so, no matter what. No matter how great the odds are, no matter how difficult or inconvenient the journey or struggle is. Willpower is staring that challenge dead in the eye, giving it a wink, and saying, *Try me!*

Having the discipline and the willpower to overcome all of the obstacles, inconveniences, and challenges that you will face provides a large stepping stone on the path to becoming your best self and being able to stand in your power. Discipline is so important. It is the strongest form of self-love. It requires you to ignore current pleasure for bigger rewards that are to come. It's loving yourself enough to give yourself everything you've ever wanted. You have to be willing to be disciplined enough to attain all that the Universe has to offer you and that is yours by divine birthright.

The next step in the willingness to overcome your adversities is to remain focused. Focus on the goal and keep your eye on the prize. It is so easy to be distracted when things aren't going your way, and it's even easier to give up. Do not ever give up, no matter how hard the times may seem. This too shall pass, and trust me when I say, if you push past what you perceive as limitation and barriers and you overcome, one day, you're going to look back and thank yourself profusely. You're going to be extremely grateful for enduring, for learning, for gaining, for loving and for evolving. You never know what life has in store for you in your future. There are so many blessings to be had if only we remain focused and believe, love and strive for what we desire. People will doubt you; there will always be naysayers along the way. Misery loves company, but don't fall victim to these people. Instead, use them as a motivating force to help you push past the doubt, the pain, the tears, and the fear. Use it to show them, the Universe, and yourself, nothing can hold you down.

Sometimes, life has a funny way of testing us, and you will be tested, time and time again, to see if what you want is really worth going for and to see how badly you really want it. Just when you think times couldn't get any tougher, sometimes the Universe says, "Hey, I heard you like growth, so I'll put some challenges on top of your challenges, so you can grow from your challenges while you grow from your growth." Sound familiar? I can say, "Yes! For sure!" In these moments, you may begin to feel so numbed with pain and start to think you can't take anymore. But you can, because you're here, and that's why you're being tested. God gives his toughest battles to his strongest warriors. The Universe will never give you something that you are not capable of taking on. Sometimes, it just takes that extra ounce of strength, discipline and willpower to remain focused and to keep your eye on the prize. Remember one day this will all be worth it. You will understand the "why?" and you will get to reap the blessings from the struggle. It will all make sense. But first, you have to keep going, and you have to pass the tests. You have to show up for yourself daily and love thyself. Rise to the occasion and prove to yourself that you are the superhero of your own movie. Where there's a will, there's a way.

Next in the concept of the willingness to overcome your adversity is having the determination and ambition to attain what it is you want. In order to be determined to accomplish something, you first must know what it is you want and why it is meaningful to you. Once your heart and soul places meaning on something that is of worth, then your heart and soul will be determined to do whatever it takes to accomplish it. You must set a clear goal for yourself, and it doesn't have to be big. It can be as simple as eliminating bread from your diet for a week. But set the goal and the intention. Express why you want it and what it means to you. You can say it out loud to yourself, to a friend, write it on a piece of paper; it doesn't matter as long as the intention is set by you.

Positive affirmations are a great way to bring about profound change into your life for the better. They are tools that can provide emotional support and encouragement as well as help manifest what you desire into the physical 3D (3rd dimensional reality). Here are a few examples of affirmations you can say to help you be more determined.

"I am full of determination."

"I am a determined person."

*"I will decide, commit, and conquer
all obstacles set before me."*

Whatever it is you choose to affirm each day, feel it in your heart and believe it to be with all your soul. If you find this to be difficult or that your mind is opposing what you are affirming, simply honor that voice and say, "Thank you, but I choose to believe I am full of determination." Eventually, you will start to believe it, because you will feel it, you will and express it wholeheartedly.

As a helpful cushion or pillow of support, don't be afraid when you fall, because you will most likely fall at some point. We all fall. It's a part of the journey, and it's a part of attaining the blessing. If this happens, simply rise and then rise again, like a phoenix from the ashes. If you are a determined person, then you will always rise upon falling, no matter what.

Between having willpower and determination, there really is no greater force other than yourself that can stop you. So, face your fears, step outside your comfort zone, stare that challenge in the eye and do not say, why me? Say, try me! Conquer your world, your wounds, your story, because it is yours to conquer and yours alone.

Accepting change is not always the easiest thing for us to do. What we think is meant for us actually isn't, and the quicker we can accept that and let go, the quicker we can call in what is meant for us. If this is the case for you, then you must be able to mourn the loss of the life you thought you had and be willing to receive with an open heart the life that is meant for you. I know this can be hard at times, especially when our hearts are attached to a certain goal or outcome. But trust that when the Universe takes something away that you thought was yours, it is for your highest and best interest, even if you can't see it or understand it in that moment. There is a lesson, and there is a reason. Your responsibility is to try to flow with it and grow with it, so that the answers may come, and they will come. Silent the mind, engage in prayer, ask for guidance because, remember, the Universe and God can only work with our free will; follow the signs, and express gratitude. You will be led on the path that is meant for you.

In the process of this change and acceptance, we're often confronted with what we're opposing or the loss of what we thought was meant for us. Just because you accept the change doesn't mean you have to like it immediately; sometimes, it takes time to accept change, especially when we perceive it as painful in the moment.

Let's take my ankle injury, for example. I hated this change; I thought I was meant to be the world's best stuntwoman, and that was it. That was my goal that I was determined and focused on. And when my ankle and career got taken away, I wasn't pleased about it; it was an emotionally, physically and mentally painful battle. But over time, I learned that everything happens for a reason. Yes, I didn't understand it at the time, but I knew that I would one day, so I kept fighting, and I kept hanging on, and I kept rising after every fall and now I conquer my Queendom.

So, you see it's ok! You don't have to like it right away, but you might as well make your best effort to try, after all you do have to live with it. It's a part of your journey. You can allow it to serve you or hinder you. Remember we all have the choice. Change can be good, and acceptance is key. The faster we accept this, the faster we can call in what's meant for us, and the faster we can enjoy our blessings.

BASIC REVIEW

In this chapter, we explored the concept of willingness and how important it is in being able to overcome your adversity and create a life of abundance.

We looked at the key factors that play a role in the willingness to overcome.

1. 'Willpower' – Willpower is the control exerted to do something or restrain impulses. To possess 'willpower' is a choice. And we can all choose to be the victim or the victor of our own lives. Have the willpower to show up and rise above any adversity you are faced with.

2. 'Focus' and keep your eye on the prize. Sometimes, life will test you to see how badly you really want something. Avoid distractions and remain focused.

3. 'Determination and ambition' are key factors in attaining what you want. You must first be clear with what you want to yourself and to the Universe. Then you must set a realistic and attainable goal, potentially with a timeline to help keep you on track. You can also affirm what it is you'd like to believe with various affirmations.

4. Accepting and applying change, even if it's not what you were hoping for. You must be able to mourn the loss of the life you thought you had in order to create room for the life that is meant for you. It's ok to not like the change at first, but eventually, you must accept it in order for things to move forward and for you to call in what is meant for you. Trust that everything happens to you for a reason and is for your highest and best interest, no matter the pain, even if you cannot see it in this present time. Trust that, one day, you will understand, so you have to have the willingness to keep fighting the good fight.

LESSON

1. Your willingness to look within at your darkness is what empowers you to change, evolve, and conquer.

2. Your capacity to learn is a gift. Your ability to learn is a skill. Your willingness to learn is a choice.

3. In order to accept the life that is meant for you, you must first mourn the loss of the life that you thought you had and be willing to overcome anything that is thrown at you.

4. Trust that everything happens for a reason, even when you are not wise enough to see it.

HOMEWORK

**In this exercise, we're going to work on setting goals. Below, I'd like you to list 3 goals that you'd like to accomplish this year. Make sure they are realistic and attainable, anything from healing a specific wound, quitting an addiction, getting a new job, reaching a certain weight, whatever it is, make sure it's attainable and realistic for you.

THIS YEAR, I WOULD LIKE TO ACCOMPLISH:

1.

2.

3.

**Next, I want you to write down 3 reasons your goals are important and meaningful to you.

GOAL 1 IS MEANINGFUL TO ME BECAUSE...

1.

2.

3.

GOAL 2 IS MEANINGFUL TO ME BECAUSE...

1.

2.

3.

GOAL 3 IS MEANINGFUL TO ME BECAUSE...

1.

2.

3.

**Next, I'd like you to write down 3 action steps you can take for each goal to make them attainable for yourself.

GOAL 1: ACTION STEPS I CAN TAKE TO MANI-FEST MY GOALS ARE:

1.

2.

3.

GOAL 2: ACTION STEPS I CAN TAKE TO MANI-FEST MY GOALS ARE:

1.

2.

3.

GOAL 3: ACTION STEPS I CAN TAKE TO MANI-FEST MY GOALS ARE:

1.

2.

3.

** Go to my website, www.rochelleokoye.com, sign up and sign in. In the members-only section, you will see a FREE DOWNLOAD for affirmations. Download the affirmations to your phone as screen savers and repeat them daily. Check back for more free and helpful material weekly.

CHAPTER FOUR

Evolve

Experiencing a life and upbringing plagued with abuse, and being abandoned and disowned by my biological parents and family was bad enough. However, my near career-ending injury and the adversity associated with it, when combined with leaving an abusive romantic relationship with a narcissist sociopath, was even more difficult. The blessing is that healing from it has undoubtedly left me in a state of being more evolved, attaining a higher level of consciousness, and able to reap in the abundance of positivity and joy from overcoming it all.

After every hardship, after every adversity, the Universe will present you with two choices, repeat or learn the lesson. More times than not, we choose to repeat until we learn, but in the end, that is how we learn. In my case, I had to endure all these hardships in order for me to evolve to the next stage of my life. I had to endure the abuse of my parents and the painful struggle of being abandoned and disowned by my very own family. Overcoming that adversity provided me the strength and resiliency to endure the journey of my permanent ankle injury. And in turn, overcoming that adversity plus the ones prior rendered me the strength and resiliency to endure a break up with a narcissist sociopath. Walking through hell, enduring and overcoming those painful hardships, led me to a life of standing in my power, living my authentic truth and creating the life of my dreams. Here I am now, sitting here, writing this book, advising you how to stand in your power and truly love yourself through self-love and deep introspection so that you can create the life of your dreams.

Your greatest teacher is your last mistake, and I can honestly say now, I have humbly learned and applied a lot of soul lessons to my life. As a result, I will never settle for anything less than what I deserve, and I know what I deserve. I have a voice, and it echoes lovingly and softly across the Universe. I have a deep love for myself because I've stared my demons in the eyes, battled them, and walked out of hell. I know my worth, and anyone who does not align with my values or well being, I simply release with love. There is no room for any toxicity or bad vibrations anymore. I know my power, and I've learned how to use it in a way that positively benefits society as well as myself. I've learned to accept the truth about who I am, as well as who each person is, both in their gifts and shortcomings. I have released my past, my fears, my old patterns of negative thinking, and I have replaced them with love, light, and positive affirmations each day. Each day, I am growing stronger in the light and wiser in the ways of the ancients, and for that, I am so extremely grateful. I'm grateful for every adversity I have faced. I love the woman I have become today and continue to grow into; I live fully in the present, yet I look forward to my future. I genuinely feel joy within my soul, and when I look back on the past and all the pain, I see the beauty in it. I understand now that light can only be understood through the wisdom of darkness.

It's our responsibility to heal ourselves so that we can be filled with the love, light, peace, joy and abundance that we were all born with. Unfortunately for some of us, it was stripped away throughout our upbringing, by society, our parents, our environment, our world. But you are personally responsible for becoming more ethical than the society you grew up in. Love thyself, heal thyself, so that you can love and help heal others. Your purpose in life is to heal and love yourself so that you can discover your soul's true purpose and then share it with the world. That's what evolving is all about, becoming the best version of yourself through overcoming your hardships and adversities.

Evolve means to develop gradually, especially from a simple to a more complex form. So if we're speaking in terms of spirituality, our goal is to evolve from a lower level of consciousness to a higher level of consciousness and vibrations. But in order to evolve so that we may one day stand in our power, there are certain things we must undertake, apply, and internalize.

No matter how hard or how painful your experiences have been, if you want to evolve to a higher-level of consciousness and call in all that you deserve and desire, then you must learn your lessons. I've mentioned several times now that the Universe will keep sending you the same lessons through different experiences until it is learned. A part of having a human experience is consciously or subconsciously choosing to learn the hard way. Oftentimes, we learn through doing, rather than being told. It's so easy for someone else to tell us what not to do. I can sit here and tell you not to date that person displaying all of those red flags, who is clearly not good for you, or don't go to that club and spend all your money on alcohol. Don't go to the casino and gamble away all of your hard-earned money every other weekday or weekend. Don't eat that junk food, exercise more, and sleep earlier. It's easy for me to tell you these things, but unless your soul is ready to learn what it came here to learn and apply, then me telling you what to do has no relevance. You have to want the change; you have to make the change. More often than not, we need to go through the negative experience, and feel the pain that that particular experience may bring before we can make a change that will serve us to our highest. Often, it's the deepest pain which empowers you to grow into your highest self.

It took me three years to gain the strength, the power, and the courage to leave my abusive relationship. I always knew in my heart and in my gut that being in it was wrong and didn't serve me to my highest in the moment. My friends and coworkers could see the horrific pain it was causing and many people made it clear to me that it was in my best interest to leave that relationship and never look back. But I had to be completely shattered and hit rock bottom, and become so broken that I had no other choice but to break myself open, heal and ascend. It didn't matter what anybody had told me at the time; I, like many others, had to learn the hard way. And these repeated experiences that kept showing up in my life in different versions of males and boyfriends were simply lessons I needed to learn. And the day that I chose to learn and say enough is enough, the day I chose to stand in my power, was the day I stopped calling in these men that continually hurt me. I continued on my healing journey. I continued to look within and to love myself and to show the Universe my new vibrations. And as a result, the Universe had no choice but to respond.

Gratitude. It is such a powerful yet humbling word. Gratitude can make sense of our past, it can bring peace for today and it creates a vision for tomorrow. I touched on gratitude in chapter 1 and continually touch on it throughout the book for a reason. Be thankful for the experience, regardless of how much pain it has caused you. Remember that being able to see the beauty in the pain and using it so that it may serve you to your highest is the blessing and the miracle in your life. After darkness always comes light.

I can continually and authentically sit here and tell you that I am grateful for the painful experience I endured with my ex, my parents and with my injury. If I didn't experience any of it, I wouldn't be who I am today. I wouldn't have learned all that I have. I wouldn't have acquired the wisdom that I need to propel me forward in my life's work and journey. I'm grateful that the pain I endured pushed me to rise to the occasion to be there for myself, to heal myself, to love myself, to help heal others and to help love others. I can only give to others what I can give to myself, and all of the adversity I have faced allowed me to create a life of diversity, and for that I am grateful. That is the miracle, to be able to turn your struggles and hardships into blessings and riches.

Intuition is the ability to understand something immediately without the need for conscious reasoning. My absolute favorite superpower is my intuition. I am a clairsentient empath. An empath is someone who can sense and feel emotions and energies of other people, animals and even objects. A person who is clairsentient can perceive energy using physical sensations, which includes an individual's aura and vibrations (words and voice). Learning to trust your intuition and using it as a guiding tool along your path is a key factor in evolving to your highest and standing in your power. I am very adamant about people learning to trust their own intuition and energy because, unlike humans, energy doesn't lie. And if you are capable of reading people's energy and trusting your intuition and the vibrations that you are receiving from others, you will save yourself a lot of drama, headaches, and unnecessary suffering.

Developing your intuition is something that can be practiced daily through meditation and grounding work, through energy work, and through practicing various intuitive developing exercises.

"There is a voice that doesn't use words. Listen."
Rumi

Over the years, I have practiced developing my intuition to the point where now I am able to read people without them even having to say a word. Does this drive some people crazy? Absolutely! We as humans tend to walk around with our masks on. We all have egos and some people wear masks in an attempt to hide it. Masks that we want others and society to perceive us as. Masks that we tend not to wear at home behind closed doors in the comfort of our own home. Japanese culture says we have 3 faces. The first face you show to the world. The second face you show to your close friends and your family. The third face, you never show to anyone and is considered the truest reflection of who you are. The third face is bare. It is our raw, genuine authentic self and soul; the third face is what we need to feel comfortable showing every day to whomever. At the end of the day, people normally expose only a small part of themselves, and generally just the part they wish to show. So, when I say it's important to trust your intuition, it's truly important to trust your intuition. Some people simply aren't who they say they are. You must be careful with the company you keep and who you trust, and the more you are in tune with yourself and your own intuition and energy, the more you are going to be in tune with others. The positive outcome to this is that no matter what anyone tells you, there is no fooling you, because energy doesn't lie.

I've mentioned before that self-love through introspection is one of the greatest gifts you can give to yourself. But I haven't discussed exactly what introspection is. Introspection is defined as the examination or observation of one's own mental and emotional processes; this can be done through self-analysis, self-examination, soul searching, self-observation, etc. Quiet introspection can be extremely profound and valuable. Honestly, it is one of the modalities that I engage in the most throughout my spiritual practice. I can and will remain contently in silence for hours on end, observing my thoughts, self, and soul. It is a way to connect within and become truly comfortable with self and silence. If you can sit with your own thoughts in silence, then you're capable of mastering your own mind, thus capable of mastering your own life.

Unfortunately, this is something a lot of humans are not comfortable doing. We become so in tune with the busyness and chaos of life and our daily routines that we become accustomed to tuning out, to escaping and distracting ourselves with external stimuli, whether that be in the form of your cell phone, the television, social media, humans (relationships), sex, drugs, alcohol, gambling, addictions - you name it. These are all symptoms of a sick society and humans that do not love themselves. As a result, we tend to engage in things and behaviours that don't serve us to our highest. If we all looked within and started to love ourselves more, not only will the love for ourselves increase, but the love for others will increase. Again, you can only give to others what you give to yourself. If you want that epic love story, you have to first look in the mirror and start with the person you see. You hear it all the time, but I'm telling you it is the only way to create positive change for yourself. Start by loving the person you see in the mirror. Dance with your shadow. Face him/her. Accept him/her. With deep introspection, you can learn to accept your precious self and receive all the love you deserve.

When you rise through adversity and conquer the love for yourself, begin to help others who are in need and striving to do the same. I believe it's important to give back and to share our stories, to own our stories, to allow our stories to empower others as well as ourselves. When you share your story and you help heal yourself, you give permission for others to heal themselves. Your story may also be the key that helps unlock someone's else prison, so it's important to share and to heal. When you heal, you're redesigning your DNA. You're stopping the intergenerational cycle prevalent in your bloodline. You're freeing yourself and future children from ancestral trauma and karmic debt. You're mastering your soul lessons and cultivating space for a flow of positive abundance.

As I mentioned in chapter 2, we rise by lifting others and there are many ways you can show up for people. Volunteering your time with a charity that aligns and resonates with your values is always a positive and impactful experience for all involved. You can show up and help others with their careers in terms of guiding and advising them on the right path. You can simply show up and be a listening ear for someone who needs it. You can possess and express empathy, communicate that powerful message of, "You are not alone." Be there for others and in return, you will find the Universe and others will be there for you. Everything is flow; let the flow of positive abundance pass through.

In the final stages of evolving into your highest, you will find yourself beginning to apply the newfound lessons to your life. You will be able to cultivate and harness a powerful source of energy that allows you to manifest what you will, and call in what you desire. You will begin to ascend to a higher level of consciousness and all that no longer serves you will fall away. If you now find the same experience repeating itself, except this time you have a different answer for it and outcome, then congratulations! You are officially moving into the next chapter of your life and mastering a soul lesson. Every next chapter of your life will demand a different you. And what you have learned in your previous chapter will help set you up for your next chapter and so on. It's like gaining and adding tools to your tool belt along the way, so you can get the job done easier as you continue. What a beautiful thing that is, which is why you must be grateful for every single experience and lesson you've learned along the way.

BASIC REVIEW

In this chapter, we looked at how becoming an evolved human being is a crucial step to standing in your power. You must evolve from the experiences and the adversity that you have faced and overcome.

We looked at the various steps to becoming evolved.

Step.1: Learn the lessons and apply them to your life; the Universe will keep sending you different experiences with the same lessons until they are learned. Listen to the signs and pass the tests when you are being called upon. Be grateful for the experiences, for they have taught you something of value and worth that you needed to learn in order to evolve your level of consciousness along your journey. There is a voice that doesn't use words, listen! Your intuition is your soul's GPS and guiding force. Energy doesn't lie! Learn to trust it. Work on trusting and developing your intuition through various exercises.

Step 2: Heal yourself. Through introspection, deep healing can take place, and you can learn to accept your precious self and receive all the love you deserve. In doing so, you're giving permission for the next person to heal and so forth. Like a chain reaction, you've given permission to all of humanity to heal and ascend.

Step 3: Empower. Empower yourself and others through sharing your story and giving back to help heal others on their path, however that may resonate with you. And then carry that wisdom and lesson that you have learned with you into your next chapter of life.

LESSON

Every next chapter of your life demands a different you.

When life is sweet, say thank you and celebrate. When life is bitter, say thank you and grow.

Your wound is most likely not your fault, but healing is your responsibility.

Trust the vibes you get; energy doesn't lie.

It's not the wound that teaches but the healing.

Intuition is the GPS of the soul; learn to trust it.

Your story could be the key that unlocks someone else's prison; don't be afraid to share it.

HOMEWORK

In this meditation exercise, we're going to work on silencing the mind and allowing ourselves to sit with any thoughts that come up and simply allow them to pass.

I want you to find a comfortable space and position. Choose either to sit or lie down in a comfortable position with no distractions surrounding you. Turn your cell phone off or silence it; turn off your television and music.

We're going to start by closing your eyes and taking some deep breaths.

Breathe in deeply through your nose and exhale 3x.

On your fourth breath in, I want you to notice any thoughts that may be coming to your mind, and I want you to honor those thoughts. Simply allow them to come. In your mind's eye, I want you to envision a beautiful illuminated basket. And in this basket, I want you to place whatever thought or worry came to your mind. I then want you to envision the basket being sent up to the sky into your Spirit Guide's, Angel's or God's hands. Envision them taking this basket from you and freeing you of your worries or distractions. I want you to say thank you and express your gratitude to your Angels, your Guides or God for their help, assistance, and love with this matter. You can repeat this for every thought that comes to your mind. When you're ready, you can take a few deep breaths, open your eyes, and return to your loving space and reality. Trust that your prayer and meditation practice has been heard by your angels, guides and God, and they will take this burden, these distractions, or fears from you, so that you may release them and allow the abundant flow of healing energy to flow freely through you.

You may return to this practice any time you are feeling overwhelmed with thoughts or burdens, worries, or fears. Release them to your Spirit Guides, to your Angels, and to God and allow them to deal with it. Trust that they are helping to assist you with things to help serve you to your highest and remember to listen to any signs or guidance that may show up for you in the physical world to help you along your journey.

CHAPTER FIVE

Responsibility

I grew up in a very abusive household. My father was born in Nigeria and survived the Biafran war as a child, also known as the Nigerian civil war. According to him he was a child soldier. As you can imagine, a lot of issues and trauma would develop from enduring a childhood like that. My father was terrifying to my 2 siblings and me while growing up. He would physically punish us for many things. If we took some juice from the fridge without asking we were physically punished for it. He would even go as far as measuring and marking down how much liquid was in the juice container. If we didn't clean something correctly, we would lose the privilege of the cleaning tool and then have to use our bare hands. Sometimes, he would be so angry and upset at us for missing a speck of dust that he would spit his food out at us, onto the floor. We then had to get down on our hands and knees beneath him and clean it up with our bare hands. He was cruel, extremely stern, strict and stubborn. My father did not love us and he expressed that often. In fact, he never expressed any loving emotions. I've never received any affection from him growing up and to this day, I have never heard the words, "I love you" from him. My father yelled a lot at the top of his lungs, and sometimes so loud and full of rage that we weren't able to understand what he was saying. He constantly threatened our lives, he would also threaten to dismember our body parts and eat them, or have us eat them. The rage that was projected from his being on a daily basis was extremely toxic and unhealthy for everyone involved. Our physical punishments were very military-like; he would dump cold water on our heads in the morning if we didn't get up when our alarm clocks went off. He would make us line up in a row and wait for our beatings one by one. He would bite us and chase us up the stairs until we were caught and beaten. He would only let us speak when spoken to and we had to reply with "yes sir" or "no sir." If we replied with an opinion or anything else it was considered "challenging" him or "talking back" and his rage would ensue.

My siblings and I were on schedules or timetables every day. Every hour, every minute was accounted for, and if we were not participating in what our schedules said we should be doing at that particular time, we would be physically punished for it. I didn't have a voice growing up. I didn't have choices and I was not allowed to make my own decisions. They were all made for me. Everything from my daily schedule, what career I was allowed to pursue, what sport I could play, to when I was allowed to speak, sleep and eat and drink, you name it, my father controlled it.

In 2006, my father disowned me from my family. He told my siblings and me that we each have 3 strikes and then we're out. According to my father, I had committed my third strike and was disowned from my family.

Now you're probably wondering what warranted me being disowned. I would love to be able to sit here and tell you a good reason... but I can't. It was Father's Day, 2006. I moved back to Vancouver from Prince George. I had graduated from University a year early at the age of 20 with a Bachelor of Science in psychology from the University of Northern British Columbia. I had a rewarding job lined up that I had attained on my own, working with children with developmental disabilities, mental illnesses, and behavioral problems. My mother called me over to their house for a "family meeting." Usually, family meetings would consist of about 3 hours of emotional, verbal and physical abuse. My father would yell with extreme rage and stare us down until we looked away like scared little dogs. This was his way of establishing power and dominance over us. Nevertheless, this particular day would be the last time I saw my biological parents in what's now been 14 years. After my father was done yelling for no particular reason, he proceeded to take out his rage in the bathroom. I saw that as my cue to leave and flee to safety, which apparently warranted my disowning. After that particular event, my father informed me that I am not worthy of being loved and if we were in Nigeria that I would be dead, they would bury me and have a funeral for me but because we live in Canada and the law does not permit that, he will let me live. With that, I was disowned and never spoken to again.

After my parents disowned and abandoned me, I felt lost and afraid, yet also free. I was finally free to make my own choices in life and pursue the life I wanted, but I also had to do that without any support. This experience was terrifying, challenging and painful. It brought on depression and suicidal thoughts and tendencies. It forced me to look within and heal some broken aspects of my inner child. It forced me to grow, evolve, and develop a sense of self I didn't have before. But at that time, I still had a long way to go on my journey before I discovered my power, knew my worth, and truly loved myself the way I deserved to be loved. This was just the beginning; it was the catalyst that set me on my spiritual journey and my path to becoming the best version of myself over the course of this lifetime.

The final and most crucial step to being able to stand in your power and manifest all that you desire is breathing and living your authentic truth and being your authentic self, all while taking responsibility for who you are and how you show up and contribute to yourself and others in this Universe. That includes taking responsibility for your healing. As I mentioned earlier, your wounds are most likely not your fault, but healing them is your responsibility. And at the end of the day, how much you love yourself will be evident through physical and emotional manifestations in your daily interactions with yourself and with others.

In a world where everyone wears a mask, it's a privilege to see a soul. At the end of the day, the goal is for each and every one of us to be walking around in the moment expressing our soul's true purpose and living our authentic truth. In order to do that, you first must be real with yourself and own the fact that you, like everyone else, may have traumas, demons, hurts, and wounds that need to be healed and attended to. You need to take responsibility for yourself and how you show up in your life. You need to own your baggage and your darkness, so that you can find and understand your light. There is no shortcut to healing, and there is no magic pill. It takes work, time, patience, and love for yourself and others along the way. Skipping steps won't get you there any faster. In fact, it will keep you blocked and in a rut because the pain will never leave until it's done teaching you what you need to know.

You need to learn to be your authentic self. There is no tricking the Universe. You are energy, and she feels everything you feel, even if you mask it with a different face every day. The Universe feels below the layers and surface of your skin. Be your authentic self.

A part of taking responsibility for who you are is owning up to the fact that you are human, and you, like everyone else, make mistakes. Mistakes are how we learn and grow if we choose to learn and grow from them. As I've mentioned before, your greatest teacher is your last mistake. Making mistakes and falling on your face is an essential part of the journey. It teaches you to have the strength, the resiliency, and the courage to pick yourself back up and try again. So when you make a mistake, admit to it. Own up to your faults. Take responsibility. Heal. When you do so, not only are you clearing your karmic debt, ending the intergenerational cycle of abuse, healing the trauma in your bloodline and DNA, learning the lesson and applying it so that it may serve you and others to the highest, you're also affirming that you love yourself enough to own up to the fact that you are not a perfect being. And a part of your purpose and journey of being on this earth is to become the best version of yourself through overcoming your trials and tribulations. Life is a school where you learn to remember what your soul already knows. Make mistakes, learn the lessons and apply them so that you may evolve into the best version of yourself.

I touched briefly on forgiveness in chapter 1. Learning to forgive is crucial if you want to stand in your power and live your authentic truth. Forgiveness for yourself and forgiveness for others. Sometimes in life, you are going to encounter people that intentionally or unintentionally wrong you and make you want to act out of alignment with love. Having emotional control and a higher level of consciousness allows you to understand that the behavior being projected onto you is merely an internalization of an issue that that person has not dealt with. Being able to forgive an individual requires you to work with your higher self and calls on the application of a higher level of consciousness.

As mentioned in chapter 1, forgiving an individual does not mean you are condoning the behavior or hurt inflicted upon you, it simply means you are setting yourself free from the hurt, and any limitations that carrying the negativity and burden from it may bring. It is your responsibility to forgive and let go. When you forgive, you are expressing vulnerability and courage. Being vulnerable is the only way to allow your heart to feel true pleasure. Being vulnerable is being authentic and being authentic is showing up in this world without your mask on. It's not easy to let go of ego and operate from love and turn the other cheek. It's much easier to seek revenge or vengeance on a person, but in doing so, you are only suffering yourself. In seeking revenge, you are attaching to the bad energy and vibrational frequency of the person that hurt you. An eye for an eye leaves both people blind. The same thing applies when projecting your energy into the world, whether it is positive or negative. Attaching to the negative only brings and attracts more negative. Releasing the negative makes room for all of the positive. That is the Law of attraction and manifestation.

Show up in this world and be your authentic self; take your mask off when you speak to people. Show the Universe who you are and be proud of the person you are becoming and evolving into every day in every way.

Operating and coming from a place of love rather than ego is the next crucial step in learning to take responsibility for yourself so that you may stand in your power. Coming from a place of love allows for an abundance of positive, loving energy to flow through you and on your path at all times.

To be able to come from a place of love, you have to be willing to peel away all of your layers and look within. You have to be willing to get to know yourself, to know your darkness, to know your light and to self-reflect, to practice introspection and learn to enjoy the journey along the way, including the highs and lows.

When you start to peel away your layers and look within, you're not always going to enjoy what you see and what comes up, and that is part of the process of healing and breaking yourself open. Be patient; be gentle with yourself when these feeling arise. It's important to honor the pain, the hurt, and the darkness.

There is no coming to consciousness without pain and suffering. People will do anything, no matter how absurd, to avoid facing their own soul. You do not become enlightened by envisioning rays of light but rather by making the darkness conscious. It's loving yourself enough to know that you deserve better and can be better. So get to know yourself and know your power; the power of your words, your silence, your mind, your body language and your energy. And then you must learn to control them.

Oftentimes, people ask me, how do you find self-love? I wish I could provide a cushy, sugar-coated answer to that question that will make everyone feel comfortable. But, if I'm to be honest, introspection and self-love is not all rainbows and butterflies. You dig, you isolate, and you ache from being lonely. You heal, you accept, you look in the mirror and see the beautiful magnificent being you were born to be. It's messy, it's uncomfortable, it's painful at times, and it's unapologetic, but it's a part of becoming who you were meant to be, and it's the most important part of calling in what is meant for you. Self-love through introspection is the greatest gift you will ever give yourself while you are here on this planet. So, give yourself the gift of self-love and start today and continue to give yourself this gift every day in every way and see how your world changes for the positive.

Another important aspect of being able to come from a place of love is having the ability to express empathy and compassion. Empathy is defined as the ability to understand and share the feelings of another. Compassion is the sympathetic pity and concern for the sufferings or misfortunes of others. If you can forgive yourself first, then you can forgive others. If you can express empathy and compassion towards yourself for the mistakes that you make, then you can express empathy, compassion and forgiveness for others. And when you can forgive others, others can forgive you. No one is perfect and we all make mistakes. We are here to learn and grow through making them, so it's only fair that you learn to forgive yourself and others.

Sometimes you don't realize how strong you are until you have to forgive someone who wronged you terribly and isn't sorry. To be able to forgive someone without receiving an apology is one of the strongest things an individual can do as far as I'm concerned. It is not an easy task, but it is very necessary for your healing and evolution. I can sit here and tell you that I have had to forgive three key players in my life who wronged me terribly without an apology. Those 3 people have taught me my greatest lessons and these experiences continually shape me into the person I am today and into the best version of myself. So what does that tell you? Oftentimes you learn your greatest lessons from your greatest challenges, and sometimes from people you thought would never hurt you. Your adversities and the hurtful experiences you encounter with others are all a part of helping to shape you into the best and highest version of yourself; oftentimes, you just don't realize it in the moment. With that being said, and as mentioned earlier, I can genuinely sit here and express to you the forgiveness and gratitude that I possess for all of the pain and hurtful experiences I've had to endure along the way.

This is the part that may be difficult for some people to ingest, but ingest I need you to do. We are responsible for every choice we make, whether you choose to believe that or not. It's important to try not to blame anyone or anything for your situation or problems. When you do that, you are saying you are powerless over your own life. And by now I hope you realize you have the power to overcome anything. An empowering step to reclaiming your life is taking responsibility for it.

Negative and bad experiences do not happen to us; they happen for us. Therefore, we can choose to be the victim or the victor of our own lives. No one is coming to save you; you must save yourself, choose to be your own superhero. Choose to take responsibility. By choosing to be the victim, you are engaging in unnecessary suffering, and as a result, you are projecting your demons and toxic behavior onto others as well as yourself. Essentially you're choosing to bleed your wounds on people who did not cut you, which in turn, will create a life of chaos, self-sabotaging, and negative vibrations. Playing the victim does not get you very far in life, and it definitely does not create a flow of positive abundance and energy. Unfortunately, in our society many people seem to enjoy playing the role of 'victim.' It is easier for you to blame someone else for your problems and make an excuse for why you are projecting toxic hurtful behavior onto others than to take responsibility for it. To point fingers and blame requires little to no effort at all, but to take responsibility requires you to look your demons in the eyes, confront them, dissect them and discover what they've been feeding on and then starve them. It requires a lot of effort and work, but in the long run, it is work that is more than worth it and will get you much farther than playing the victim and remaining small.

Sometimes people are afraid to heal because they've built their entire identity around the trauma they've experienced. They've held on to that story for so long that they have no idea who they are outside of that trauma, and that alone can be terrifying. The fact that the trauma elicits a certain response or attention from others is also a part of the victim mentality and why some people prefer to remain victims to their experiences. Sadly, some people enjoy the attention that trauma can bring from others, whether it be good or bad. But your negative and traumatic experiences are not an excuse to be a negative and hurtful person. Your negative childhood experiences aren't an excuse to be a negative, hurtful person. Your manifestations of abuse and negative relationships aren't an excuse to be a negative, hurtful person. We all have our negative and traumatic experiences, and as I've said before, you can either let it define you or you can grow from it. Victim or Victor? You have the free will to decide. We all operate with free will. The choice is always yours, and the beautiful thing is you can decide at any moment to change your story and how you show up for yourself and others.

On the other hand, taking responsibility, owning the fact that you have wounds and owning the fact that you are the victor and can overcome any adversity, allows space for healing and in turn gives permission for others to heal. It's all about how you show up in this world for yourself and for others. The only way to show up with your authentic love and light is to heal your wounds through self-love and introspection. Self-love is soul retrieval; it's how you find your authentic self. So ask yourself today, how are you showing up for yourself and others?

Oftentimes we can get so caught up in thinking about and working on what we want that when we don't get it or we receive the opposite, we become quite upset or frustrated about it. Bear in mind that oftentimes adversity is put on your path to prepare you for what you asked for. Sometimes what you want and when you want it doesn't always align. Maybe you're not ready for what you think you want in the moment, therefore the Universe might serve you some more adversity to help shape you into the person you need to be in order to maintain what it is you're about to call in or want. Trust that whatever is served to you in whatever moment is put there to help you evolve into your highest and possibly prepare you for exactly what you asked for.

The responsibility you take on of healing your wounds through self-love creates a powerful and loving impact on the world and all of humanity. When you can achieve this, you have learned to stand in your power, you have learned to live, breathe and speak your authentic truth and be your authentic self. You may have discovered your soul's true purpose; you are now setting boundaries that serve you and others to the highest. You have learned to create and harness an abundance of positive, joyous free-flowing energy in and around your world. As the famous Australian Aboriginal Proverb says, "We are all visitors to this time, this place. We are just passing through. Our purpose here is to observe, to learn, to grow, and to love and then we return home."

At the end of it all, your journey is between you and God. When you're on your deathbed, you're not going to be thinking, *Maybe I should have bought that boat or that house.* You're going to be thinking about how you made others feel, how you showed up for yourself and for others in this world. As Maya Angelou said, whether you like it or not, people will forget what you said and forget what you did, but they always seem to remember how you made them feel. Understand that the true currency of the earth is not money, but rather, energy. Are you rich? Or are you in debt? If you find yourself in debt, then you have the choice to turn things around for the positive and put the loving work into yourself to get out of it.

While you're here on this earth plane, it is your responsibility to love yourself enough to heal your wounds, to love others, and to accept them both in their shortcomings and gifts, to stand in your power, speak your authentic truth, set your boundaries, be your authentic self, discover and share your soul's true purpose, grow into the best version of yourself through your trials and tribulations and create all of the magic that is yours to create by divine birthright.

People will throw bricks at you. That is a part of life, learning, and being a soul that is having a human experience. Whatever you do, do not stoop to their level and throw them back. Instead, try to rise above and collect them all. Use them to build your empire. I have taken every single brick that has been thrown at me, allowed myself the time, patience, and self-love to heal my wounds, and continue to heal, as it's a lifelong journey. I've laid a firm foundation and continue to build upon my empire. My castle is now made out of the beautiful, illuminated, polished bricks that were once tarnished and tried to destroy me.

Now, I can genuinely say my castle can never be knocked down, no matter what. The foundation is made out of the greatest gift we can ever give to ourselves: self-love. A gift that I attained through overcoming adversities and hardships, a gift that no one can ever take away from me, a gift that I had to experience in order to attain wisdom. It is invaluable, and it is indestructible, and it's left me with a knowing that, in my future, all things that are thrown at me shall turn to ashes and light a path under my feet. To all the people along the way who hurt me, betrayed me, abandoned me or rejected me, you unknowingly pointed me in the direction of my own north star. Without the messes, I wouldn't have a message. You taught me more than you could ever take from me, and for that I am forever grateful.

From this point forward continuing on your journey, remember, not everything is handed to everyone in life. Sometimes you have to face adversity and you have to learn the lesson before you can elevate yourself to the next level. Sometimes you have to go through these challenges in order to live and learn and evolve to get to where you want to be. Bad things don't happen to you, they happen for you; all for your soul's evolution. Take responsibility and heal yourself. Find your soul's true purpose and then be brave enough to share it with the world. We all create our own realities and we all have magic within us. You have to tap into your magic. You have to stand in your power. You live and you learn. So don't fear the adversity, face it. Face your demons, conquer them, love thyself.

BASIC REVIEW

In this chapter, we looked at how important it is to take responsibility for your life in order to be able to stand in your power.

In order to take responsibility for your own life, you have to be willing to be your authentic self and take your mask off when you speak to people.

You have to be able to express forgiveness for yourself and for others. When you're able to forgive yourself for your mistakes and wrongdoings, you are able to forgive others for the same thing. We are all human. Making mistakes is inevitable and part of the human journey. The faster we can forgive, the faster we return to love.

I explained that a part of taking responsibility for yourself is the importance of being able to operate from a place of love rather than ego.

In order to be able to operate from love and not ego, you have to be willing to love yourself enough to start the process of self-reflection and to look within. Engage in deep introspection and truly love thyself. You must express empathy and compassion for yourself and for others.

I expressed how we all have the choice to be the victim or victor of our own lives. And how we must take responsibility for the fact that we are the creator of our own realities; therefore, we are responsible for every choice we make and the outcome that ensues. Choosing to be your own superhero and taking responsibility for yourself, for your wounds, for your healing, for your choices will only serve you to your highest in the long run and is a part of how you create the life you desire.

Owning your story is an important part of taking responsibility for yourself, as well as healing yourself and giving permission for others to heal themselves. Own your story and be proud of your evolution and progress.

The responsibility you take on of healing your wounds through loving yourself creates a powerful and loving impact on the world and all of humanity.

LESSONS

Oftentimes, the wound is not your fault, but healing it is your responsibility.

No one is coming to save you; you must save yourself. We all have the choice to be the victim or the victor.

There is no such thing as luck. Everything you have you co-created with the Universe.

Love is never outside of us; it is always within. Self-love is the greatest gift you can give to yourself.

Take responsibility for yourself because no one is going to take responsibility for you. If you can do this, you will develop a hunger to manifest and accomplish your dreams.

HOMEWORK

Today, you are going to take responsibility for the healing of your wound(s). You're going to begin the journey of healing whatever trauma or negative experience or energy you may be holding on to that is no longer serving you or that simply needs to be released so that you may call in all that abundance that you deserve and that is yours by divine birthright.

A.) I want you to write down one wound or trauma that you would like to try to heal or release from this point forward:

_____

B.) In this exercise, you're going to write a letter to the person you feel has wronged you or caused you pain, grief or trauma, whom you would like to release, so that you may begin the process of healing. You can choose to send the letter or burn it and release it into the Universe. Both serve the purpose equally. For example, you may have had an abusive mother or father who neglected you and didn't treat you well. You can write your letter addressing them either separately or together. In this letter, you are going to express the pain that they have caused. You may recall certain events or memories. As you're writing and recalling these memories, certain emotions may be elicited. Allow them to come and honor them as they do, knowing full well that this is a part of the healing journey. We allow the sadness to flow through us and out of us so that we can create room for joy and the abundance of positive energy. As you're writing the letter, I want you to express the pain and the memories that you recall. As you near the end of the letter, I want you to express the lessons that it has taught you. I want you to try to find the positive in the negative, the beauty in the pain. As the letter comes to a close, you can choose to release them from your life or make amends and heal the bond if it is severed. Only you know what you have to do with each relationship to serve you to your highest. Not all relationships are capable of being reconciled, and sometimes, we are better off loving people from afar. Other times, the relationship is salvageable and can be reconciled if both parties are willing to take responsibility and come from a place of love and understanding. If this is the case, you may find that this relationship serves you to your highest, and I encourage forgiveness, growth and reconnection of the severed bond and relationship. No one is sent by accident, and there are no coincidences; everyone is sent to you for a reason. It's up to you to determine what that may be and if it's worth keeping. After you have finished the letter, you can choose to send it to the person you have addressed it to, or you can choose to burn it or throw it out, but when doing so, do it with love and envision and feel the release of this person and the burden, the heaviness, the hurt that has been weighing you down. Feel that weight being lifted off you as you release the letter.

C.) In this 10-minute meditation, I want you to sit or lie down in a comfortable position. I want you to close your eyes and take 5 deep breaths, inhaling and exhaling through the nose. I want you to begin to visualize your inner child and see him or her. They may be crying or upset. Their back may be turned, and I want you to feel the pain, the sadness, and the hurt that they may be experiencing and feeling. I want you to approach your inner child gently and slowly, with so much love in your heart. You might want to reach out a hand or bend to their level and give them a hug. Assure them that you are here now to help them, to love them, and to support them on your journey together. To help heal them so they can be a healthy, whole loving adult. I want you to envision embracing your inner child. You both are connected and bonded in an infinite stream of love, transpiring through a hug that is deep and meaningful and so precious. Your inner child can feel all the love you have to give him or her, and she/he begins to smile and grasp you even tighter. You begin to feel so much joy overcoming your body, and you begin to smile.

The two of you embrace in an ever-lasting tight hug, while you're laughing and being filled with an abundant flow of unconditional love and joy. You can release each other now and just enjoy the moment of being in each other's loving presence. You may choose to dance, or skip, or run, play together, whatever makes you feel happy and light.

You stop and look at each other, and you come down to his or her level. I want you to look your inner child in the eyes and tell them how much you love them. Tell them that you are here for them now. You have shown up. You are going to listen to their needs and what they want, and you will help and do what you need to do to be the protective, loving adult that your hurting inner child needs. I want you to take a moment and have this conversation with them and feel the emotions that come to the surface as you speak from your authentic, loving higher self. Envision your inner child receiving your message with love and trust. When you're finished delivering your message, I want you to embrace your inner child one last time and say your goodbyes. When you're ready, I want you to take 3 deep breaths and on the 3rd, slowly open your eyes.

D.) I encourage you to use any of the tools you have been given in this book as part of your daily practice on your journey to standing in your power, living your authentic truth and creating the life of your dreams.

About the Author

Rochelle Okoye is a Best-selling Author, Speaker, Professional Hollywood Stunt Woman and Actress and Co-Owner of Tristar Vancouver Martial Arts. Rochelle is best known for her roles alongside some of Hollywood's biggest names. She is one of the industry's most well known Stunt Women and Actresses with over 100 credits to her name. Some of her major motion feature roles include: starring as Storm's Stunt Double and Famine in the X-men Franchise, Deadpool, Twilight, War for Planet of the Apes, Underworld, and The Predator just to name a few. She's worked on countless TV shows, acting and stunt doubling such as: Arrow, Supergirl, Batwoman, Altered Carbon, The Flash, The 100, Wayward Pines, Unreal, Travelers, The Crossing and many more.

Rochelle teaches film fighting to aspiring actors across the country in workshops, classes, seminars and private training sessions and has been the featured model for various international brand companies such as Lululemon and the Steve Nash Fitness World Franchise.

Rochelle has been featured in 'The Hollywood Reporter' and 'Variety: Below the Line Impact Report,' as well as featured in various international articles and interviews.

Rochelle delivered an extremely successful Tedx Talk in November 2018 that resulted in a standing ovation from a sold-out crowd on the topic, 'The Power of overcoming your adversities.' She has been asked to speak to thousands of youth across America and Canada on the importance of following your dreams and overcoming adversity.

Rochelle attained a Bachelors of Science degree in Psychology from the University of Northern British Columbia in 2006. She graduated among her peers a year early, both at high school and University. After completion of her degree and graduation, Rochelle worked with and counseled children and youth with developmental disabilities, mental illnesses and behavioral issues in and outside the school system for several years.

Rochelle fulfilled a very successful 13-year international gymnastic career from a young age while growing up. She was nominated and awarded for the Top Sports Person in the UK for her age Category, two years in a row. She was the 3x National Great Britain Gymnastic Champion and Rochelle was also a 2000 Olympic hopeful, where her goals fell shy due to the International Gymnastic Federation (FIG) rule change. And at the very young age of 13, the BBC filmed and aired a Documentary on her gymnastics goals of reaching the 2000 Olympics called, 'Going for Gold'.

In an effort to keep challenging herself physically and mentally, Rochelle journeyed into the world of martial arts; training and competing in the disciplines of Brazilian Jiu Jitsu, Muay Thai and fulfilling an amateur and professional Boxing career. Rochelle also attained a Personal Training Diploma and began helping others achieve their fitness goals. Rochelle is now the co-owner of a successful and very well known MMA gym located in Vancouver, BC, Canada known as Tristar Vancouver Martial Arts. It is home to some of Canada's greatest MMA talent and home to UFC athletes and National Champions. Tristar Vancouver Martial Arts is also the National Training Center for the Canadian National MMA team.

After a life filled with painful challenges, hardships and adversity, Rochelle has found an inner power and formula to not only overcome but to succeed on a scale most foresee as unattainable. Rochelle has acquired wisdom and knowledge that can only be gained through a life of experience and through that she believes has a responsibility and calling to give back and help others on their journey. Rochelle helps heal and motivate others to strive for what they want and attain it no matter how big the dream and no matter how dark the path or past. She teaches others that there is beauty in pain and that light can only be understood through the wisdom of darkness. Through deep introspection and self-love, we are all capable of becoming the best versions of ourselves.

Rochelle Okoye can be reached at rochelleokoye.com